Queen o

D1577868

books, videos, ...
and more, that help you nurture your
faith and

Find your way Home.

At **www.QueenofPeaceMedia.com**
sign up for our newsletter to receive new content.

You can browse through
**Queen of Peace Media's YouTube channel for help
in safely navigating our tumultuous times.**

To be notified of our new YouTube videos,
see www.youtube.com/c/queenofpeacemedia
or go to YouTube.com and search for Queen of
Peace Media, then click "Subscribe" and the
bell icon (top right of the screen).

Visit Us on Social Media. Like & Follow us!
Facebook: www.facebook.com/QueenofPeaceMedia
Instagram: www.instagram.com/QueenofPeaceMedia
Pinterest: www.pinterest.com/catholicvideos

ABOUT THE AUTHOR

Christine Watkins (www.ChristineWatkins.com) is an inspirational Catholic speaker and author. Her books include

the Catholic best-seller, *Full of Grace: Miraculous Stories of Healing and Conversion through Mary's Intercession*, and the highly acclaimed, #1 Amazon best-sellers: *The Warning: Testimonies and Prophecies of the Illumination of Conscience (El Aviso: Testimonios y Profecías sobre la Illuminación de Consciencia); Of Men and Mary: How Six Men Won the Greatest Battle of Their Lives (Hombres Junto a María: Así Vencieron Seis Hombres la Más Ardua Batalla de Sus Vidas);* and *Transfigured: The Patricia Sandoval Story (Transfigurada: La Historia de Patricia Sandoval).* She is the author of *In Love with True Love: The Unforgettable Story of Sister Nicolina,* and the upcoming — if not already here — *Marie Julie Jahenny: Prophecies and Protection for the End Times.*

Watkins has reintroduced an ancient and powerful Marian Consecration to the world, which is resulting in extraordinary graces for parishes and people who go through it: *Mary's Mantle Consecration: A Spiritual Retreat for Heaven's Help,* with the accompanying *Mary's Mantle Consecration Prayer Journal (El Manto de María: Una Consacración Mariana para Obtener Ayuda Celestial* y *El Manto de María: Diario de Oración para la Consagración).* For details, see the end of this book.

Formerly an anti-Christian atheist living a life of sin, Watkins began a life of service to the Catholic Church after a miraculous healing from Jesus through Mary, which saved her from death. Her story can be found in the book, *Full of*

Grace. Before her conversion, Watkins danced professionally with the San Francisco Ballet Company. Today, she has twenty years of experience as a keynote speaker, retreat leader, spiritual director, and counselor—with ten years working as a hospice grief counselor and another ten as a post-abortion healing director. Mrs. Watkins lives in Sacramento, California with her husband and three sons.

ISBN: 978-1-947701-13-7

WINNING
THE BATTLE
FOR YOUR SOUL

*Jesus' Teachings through
Marino Restrepo:
A St. Paul for Our Times*

Introduced, compiled, and edited by
Christine Watkins

CONTENTS

FOREWORD

by María Vallejo-Nágera

One of the most widely read authors in all of Spain and Latin America

Dear reader,

My name is María Vallejo-Nágera. I was born in Spain, and I am an author of novels based on true events. . . fourteen thus far, in which God always plays a formidable role. The Lord has been my Helper, guiding me through the complicated and upending twists of my literary path.

This foreword poses a challenge for the simple reason that it is a gift for me. I've had yet to be asked to write about a friend whom I admire as much as Marino Restrepo! Our friendship is true; it is based on the love that we both share for Jesus Christ, Our Lord, and I sincerely believe that we were introduced by His Mother.

The first time I heard Marino's name was in the year 1999. News of my testimony of conversion to Catholicism had become so public and wide-spread that Franciscan priests as far away as Bosnia-Herzegovina asked me speak at the Medjugorje Youth Festival, a conference filled with the Holy Spirit and attended by an impressive number of people—about 80,000.

My Catholic faith had burst into my life a few years earlier, like a nuclear bomb. Even though I had always been Catholic in name, almost from birth (baptized within the first month of my life), my heart had never experienced intimacy with Jesus. I can explain. . .

Spain is a very unique country. The vast majority of us are Catholic, but my generation (I was born in 1964) grew up in an environment of "social" religion. Our schools were Catholic, as were our families, and we lived ensconced in a Catholic world that taught us religious norms and plenty of theology, but little about love and closeness to God.

So while my family and teachers had mastered the Catechism by memory and knew the theological foundations of our faith, their souls had not learned to converse with the living God. I went in a forced manner to Sunday Mass, deeply bored, without understanding its theological principles, meaning, or supernatural power and richness. Today, twenty years after my conversion, I understand that to study Jesus is essential, but far more important is to love Him, know Him, speak to Him from the heart.

Where I grew up, in Madrid (the capital of Spain and my home), everyone was baptized because the Church was intrinsically linked to the state. Nearly my entire generation of Spaniards received the Sacrament of Confirmation, and after falling in love, young couples married in the Catholic Church, entering into Holy Matrimony more due to social impulse than for any other studied reason. Nowadays, Spain has changed its criterion, and nothing is the same anymore. . . . Couples divorce by the millions, and the population that chooses to marry in the Church lies shy of fifty percent. Faith is lukewarm, and in large measure, almost nonexistent.

With this panorama as my backdrop, I was invited in 2000, by a friend, to visit a little village lost between the Bosnian mountains, called Medjugorje. By then, I was married and living in London with three small children. I protested with a thousand sorry excuses for not going. But on May 9, I found myself there, cajoled and finally pushed to go by an . . . Anglican! I still don't understand how my friend, Kristina, managed to convince me. Somehow, the voice of God made itself felt in my heart, and by a pure miracle, not without complaint, I succumbed.

The outcome of that pilgrimage to Medjugorje was that the Lord captured my heart. My conversion, a three-second, supernatural encounter with God's Heart, was monumental. I was lifted from the abyss of a terrible agnosticism directly into the sublime embrace of God. The Lord captivated my poor, stained soul, so much so, that upon my return to London, I was no longer the same person.

In the years that followed, I simply could not keep myself from sharing the love I had found. Books flowed from my heart with the power of faith. I cannot count how many hundreds of presentations and travels I have undertaken for the sake of the Lord. . . All of my writings, my novels, and articles, have been dedicated to God's Glory, because nothing matters to me more than loving Christ.

Come August of 2010, I returned to Medjugorje and took the stand. I can vividly recall my fright over seeing an immense sea of tens of thousands of young people, so quiet, so attentive to my words. To them, I told my story, as if sharing with close friend. . . I spoke of how my writing before my conversion was filled with sarcasm toward priests and the Church. I shared the experience of my first Mass in Medjugorje, when I blocked out the preaching and instead, took pictures. And then I explained to them how when I was outside of St. James Church, walking alongside the lines of confessionals, joking with my friends, I felt an urge to look up. Suddenly, an invisible divine arrow pierced my heart with a strong, extravagant, and ecstatic love. In that moment of just three seconds of earthly time, God's voice said to me from eternity, "This is how much I love each and every one of you around the world." This overwhelming feeling of love turned to pain as I suddenly understood how seriously I had mistreated my Catholic parents, and my faith, and God. I wanted to hide, but He spoke again: "Please tell the world that there is a God, and that God loves everyone."

I told the multitudes of young people that it was a simple command, but being confused and young, I didn't dare reveal my mystical experience to anyone until six months later. That person was my spiritual director, Fr. Michael O'Malley, who had accompanied the pilgrims on my trip to Medjugorje in 2000. I felt like I was divulging a grand secret, but Fr. O'Malley wasn't at all surprised: "You are simply one of the many conversions of Medjugorje. You must understand that Medjugorje is the lung of the world."

When my talk ended, I walked away from the podium with a huge sigh. Now I could breathe easily. I had done my job, and I thought I had done it well.

That night, after a grueling and exhausting, but exciting day, I was invited to dinner at one of the local homes. The families of Medjugorje are so full of God, humble, and generous. . . the town of Medjugorje so imbued with the Holy Spirit, so different from the big European cities I was accustomed to. It was during that dinner, while surrounded by joyful pilgrims and basking in the hospitality of a beautiful Medjugorje family, in a Marian place of pilgrimage, that I first heard about Marino Restrepo.

"He's Colombian," they shared with me. "And today, after your testimony, he gave his." Oh, how I wished I had known that detail some hours before! I wondered how the Franciscans had not told me about this man who had been kidnapped by Colombian guerrillas. . . and while held in captivity in the Amazon jungle, fearful that the terrorists were about to kill him, he suddenly underwent an extraordinary mystical experience—the illumination of his conscience. Not only did his life of sin pass before his internal eyes, but overnight, God infused his soul with divine knowledge, a singularly unique gift in all of known Christendom. . .

I learned of how Marino's life was miraculously saved, and how, thanks to God's protective love, he is still among us today. . . and his testimony had followed mine by minutes! The story they told me, amidst the emotional astonishment and tears of some of those present, engraved itself in my mind. "This exceptional, mystical, and Holy Spirit-filled testimony is not known in Spain," I thought. That night, an immense desire to meet Marino was born in my heart. . .

Shortly before dawn the next day, I had to leave for Madrid, which prevented me from seeking out a Franciscan at the parish to help me contact this wonderful man I had missed. Well, I thought. "I am going to trust my God . . . If Jesus so wishes, one day I will meet Marino Restrepo."

Upon my return to my country, I asked around. . . No one seemed to know or have heard of the man from Colombia whose fascinating encounter with God and divine words of wisdom stirred the souls of his audiences across the globe, and whose infused knowledge from God was of such volume and magnitude, that his well of subjects never runs dry. No priest, no parish in my country, could give me information. Thus, somewhat crestfallen, I traveled to the south of Spain for a summer vacation with lifelong friends.

Not three days of my stay had passed when a friend invited me to dinner at her house. "I want to introduce you to a wonderful married couple from Peru," she said. "They are ambassadors now in Spain, and the wife wants to meet you because she knows of your novels and admires your work." My heart began beating with expectation, and I attended in high spirits. The evening turned out to be very enjoyable: the guests were accomplished professionals, a lovely, cultured, happy couple. During dessert, the ambassador's wife turned to me and said abruptly, "María, dear, have you heard of Marino Restrepo? He's a great Colombian convert. . . He is a friend of mine. If not, you should certainly meet him some day because something tells my heart that you two are going to be great companions in God's adventures."

I almost fell off my chair. . .

God's business is like that. I call such moments "God-incidences." As soon as she mentioned Marino, a cascade of questions poured out of my mouth with such unstoppable force that I thought they would flood the table. "I want to know everything about Marino Restrepo!" I exclaimed. She fed me information, as best she could, as I fired questions at her like bullets. When I finally noticed the time, it was two in the morning. I had made a new friend in God and received a message that echoed in my heart, announcing that soon, very soon, I would meet Marino personally.

That night, as I lay down in bed, saying my night prayers, I asked the Lord not to delay long. I desperately desired to meet Marino as a new and very special friend! I longed to express my many doubts and receive answers from this man who had met God in the most extraordinary way. Who would be so foolish as to not want to meet and talk with such a person?

When the summer came to an end, I returned to Madrid and adapted to the normal routine of home life, work, and my children's schooling. Time flew by, but my burning desire to meet Marino Restrepo stayed. One morning, I received an unexpected phone call from a devoted Catholic friend. "Have you heard the news?" he asked. "A man from Colombia is going to come to Madrid to give a talk about his conversion. . . Apparently, Colombian guerillas kidnapped him, took him into the deep jungle, and made him suffer terrible things. They had plans to assassinate him, but the Lord appeared to him. . ." I smiled.

"Ah, my Jesus!" I whispered. "You and your Mother never fail. . ."

I quickly jotted onto a piece of paper the place, date, and time of the talk. How nervous and joyful I was! A little parish, nestled in the middle of Old Madrid (my favorite place!) had invited Marino to give his testimony. My soul anticipated something as big and important as the birth of a new and powerful friendship between Christian siblings.

When the day finally arrived, I rushed to the parish to find a tiny church filled with few people. What sadness I felt to see that hardly anyone in my city had heard of the impressive story of Marino's salvation! Despite feeling somewhat disappointed, alone, and shy, I took my seat in the front pew with eager ears and attentive eyes, grateful to God for having arranged a time and place for Marino to come and minister to us.

When Marino walked in, joy beamed from his face. He did not seem upset by the low turnout . . . at all! "The Lord is the one who invites the audience to my talks! If we are few, it is because Jesus, my Lord, has decided so!" he exclaimed with a wide smile.

From that moment on, everything flowed with sweet, tender perfection, the kind that only comes from the presence of the Holy Spirit. Marino began his passionate story, with memories of his earlier atheism, his fearless youth riddled with sin, his horrible kidnapping, the pain and terror of seeing his sinfulness before the omnipresence of Jesus, and his miraculous and unexpected liberation from the hands of his torturers.

From my pew, I listened with total fascination. The Holy Spirit floated in every corner, every nook of the church. Tears began to flow from the corner of my eyes, as a deep and true admiration for Marino was planted in my heart.

At the end of the talk (thanks to the small crowd!) I was able to approach Marino. We chatted with ease. After a while, we were in the company of a few attendees when Marino informed me that he did not have transportation to return to his hotel. Night had long begun, and outside was pouring rain. Without hesitating, I offered myself to be his private taxi driver! He got into my MINI car, awkwardly. . . How much we laughed! Not everything fit: either he would enter, or his large suitcase would enter, but not both. In the end, after some shoving, we were able to organize ourselves, and I drove him to his hotel.

That spectacular night, a friendship like brother and sister began under the precious love of our Lord, Jesus, and the tenderness of our Mother.

We have shared adventures, information, and conference podiums. We have followed each other's tracks, and sometimes we have lost them, given our complicated and duty filled lives. But the Lord always brings us together again.

It is Jesus Who directs our friendship, and many times I find myself telephoning Marino to ask, sometimes beg for his help in steering my path toward Christ.

As the globetrotter for God that he is, Marino has returned many times to Spain and now lives with one foot here and one there. In his journey as a missionary evangelizer, he has suffered through many vicissitudes: insults, jail, persecution, mockery, demonic attacks. . . But nothing seems to shake his immeasurable trust in Jesus, his immense love for the Blessed Virgin Mary, the Catholic Church, his great respect for priests, and his sincere loyalty to the sacraments and the magisterium. Marino is a tremendous apostle. Like Mary Magdalene, his repentance was deep and sincere, thus his path of sin was left behind, and all has been forgiven by Jesus. Marino is a living icon of trust the mercy of a God Who does not abandon anyone, even the staunch sinner, miles from grace.

My advice for you, dear reader, is "Listen to him!" Our brother, Marino, can teach us a great deal, and this little book is AN AUTHENTIC JEWEL OF GOD. Through him, Jesus wishes to open our eyes to many essential, spiritual realities, and the unseen battle that surrounds us. The words of God that Marino is able to transmit are not prepared by his own intellect. His works are based on prayer and trust. The Holy Spirit simply pours through him, and a torrent of words flows from his mouth with wisdom and understanding far beyond human capacity. In short, Marino's teachings do not come from great theological studies or university diplomas; they come from God. I was amazed to discover that he prepares nothing for his talks. He stands before his audience, says a prayer, opens the Bible to a random page, reads aloud an unplanned passage before him—and then the Lord takes over. He would have tired long ago, he says, if he had to use his mind to think through and create in advance the hundreds of thousands of presentations he has given.

Therefore, I assure you that this precious book, *Winning the Battle for Your Soul*, is not enough to explain the awesome spiritual power that shakes Marino's soul when he begins each of his ministries. But it is the beginning of a highly recommended exploration of the richness that this impressive case of mysticism in the twenty-first century contains. I also encourage you to read Marino's soul-shaking testimony of conversion in the phenomenal #1 best-selling book, *The Warning: Testimonies and Prophecies of the Illumination of Conscience*. You will not regret it.

My advice is that you now begin this prize of a book with the heart of a child, with a humble soul, and prepare yourself in prayer to receive some of the most amazing secrets of our God.

With love, always,

MARIA VALLEJO-NÁGERA

My website can be found here: www.mariavallejonagera.com, and my conversion story here: https://youtu.be/Ap6sEc6g05Y.
Contact: oficina@mariavallejonagera.com

INTRODUCTION

There is simply no story like that of Marino Restrepo. Born in Colombia to a large, well-to-do family of coffee growers, Marino's early life was steeped in the Catholic faith and Colombian culture, where his family remained. But Marino moved away from his roots, not only physically but spiritually. First, his family sent him to Bogotá to finish high school. It was the 1960s, and he was fourteen. Taking advantage of his sudden freedom, he discarded the "trappings" of the Sacrament of Reconciliation, and shortly thereafter, the Mass. Then at sixteen, he met an American girl, a hippy with bright blue eyes, who introduced him to all she knew about sex and marijuana.

Having flung open a few doors to the demonic, Marino succumbed easily to the lure of harder drugs and the "enlightened" practices of the New Age movement. Worldly success and wild women threw themselves at him, and he embraced them all in return. In time, Marino landed in Hollywood, California. There he stayed for twenty-nine years, climbing the ladder of the entertainment industry into the life of a record producer and the belief that he was the coolest guy in town.

Then one Christmas Eve night in Colombia, when he was home for a visit in 1997, everything changed. Marino was kidnapped by Colombian FARC guerillas. Tied up with rope and blind-folded, he was led by his captors for miles into the hidden depths of the Amazon jungle. When they finally stopped, he was tossed into a dilapidated shed filled with bats, excrement, cobwebs, and thousands of crawling insects that bit him mercilessly from head to toe.

Just days into his hellish captivity, God came to Marino. As night closed in and the bats awoke, spreading their wings to take flight in the darkness, the Lord guided him through an illumination of his conscience. Unaware and disbelieving that God even existed, Marino was shown his entire life of sin. Then he was taken before the Tribunal of God, where his sentence for eternity was hell. As he sank into a horrifying web of the demons he had lived most of his life, yet whom he was seeing for the first time, his Mother in Heaven pleaded with him to accept her Son's extended hand of Mercy. Marino had lived in such grave sin for so many years, his conscience had degraded so precipitously, that he found this offering of merciful love terribly difficult to accept. But he did.

What followed was even more extraordinary. Marino received a signal grace that few, if any, have ever known. In the span of one night, God infused his soul with a vast amount of divine knowledge of which he hasn't forgotten a drop.

When dawn came, Marino was an entirely different man. It was not his time to die. After nearly a half year in captivity, he was mysteriously released. In time and after much healing, he was called upon, to his surprise, to tell his story and to begin sharing the teachings that God had given him. Today, Marino's greatest desire is to spread the love and knowledge of Jesus Christ and His Church to the far corners of the Earth until his very last breath. At the Lord's request, he has traveled to over 100 countries sharing his testimony and the teachings he received during his overnight encounter with the living God.

The teachings in this book come from Jesus, not from Marino Restrepo. Other than scattered lessons, quickly forgotten, from his youth, Marino never learned his Catholic faith. He never took a course in theology, never studied the Church's teachings, never opened a Bible. He never watched religious programming on television or fraternized with Christians. Marino's sojourn into spirituality was focused solely on learning and spreading New Age and occult beliefs and scoffing at "outdated Catholic nonsense." (If you would like to read Marino Restrepo's complete and spell-binding story, it can be found in the best-selling book: *The Warning: Testimonies and Prophecies of the Illumination of Conscience.*[1])

The Lord also called Marino to found a fraternity of lay missionaries, called the Pilgrims of Love,[2] committed to the urgent task of the new evangelization, help for the poor, and the revitalization of the Church through prayer and faithfulness to its magisterial teachings. On June 16th, 2011, the Ecclesiastical Court, headed by Cardinal Ruben Salazar Gomez, approved the Pilgrims of Love Foundation as part of the Archdiocese of Bogotá, in Marino's home country of Colombia, where he resides.

This little book contains some of the most edifying and invaluable gems of wisdom that unfold the mystery of who we really are as human beings. They are taken, synthesized, and edited from a few of Marino's talks and his book, *From Darkness into the Light.*[3] You will learn more about what it means to possess a soul, further understand the influences of your past and your ancestry, explore untold blessings of the sacraments, and emerge equipped with spiritual weapons for the fight for salvation—a battle each of us must undergo in order to reach heaven, our true home.

This, however, is just the tip of the iceberg. You are also encouraged to watch videos of Marino's talks, searchable online in English and Spanish, and to absorb what you can of his mind, while there is still time. Marino Restrepo is hailed as a St. Paul for our century, and to miss his teachings, which are not his own, would be to deprive yourself of a mystical map for the journey of life.

---

[1] Christine Watkins, *The Warning: Testimonies and Prophecies of the Illumination of Conscience*—Second Edition with the Imprimatur of the Church (Sacramento, CA: Queen of Peace Media, 2020).
[2] www.marinorestrepo.com, Peregrinos del Amor (pilgrims of love), accessed August 29, 2020.
[3] Marino Restrepo, *From Darkness into Light* (Glendale, CA: Mission "Pilgrims of Love," 2003).

CHAPTER 1

The Lord's Teachings

After Jesus guided me through the illumination of my conscience, He began to lead me through extensive teachings. The Lord spoke about my life, humanity, salvation, the Church, angels and saints, Our Lady, good and evil, the Ten Commandments, what He called the "soul's economy," and so much more. The state I was in is very difficult to describe. The only way I can think to express this phenomenon would be to say that everything He spoke of materialized in front of my eyes and was infused into my heart.

Words do not allow me to touch the surface of perfection, peace, and absolute wisdom in which Jesus' teachings took place, and I will never be able to measure them. If I were to live another hundred years, I would not be able to convey even the minimum of all the Lord shared. I had never studied in books or read anything of what He taught me, or heard it from the people around me. Everything was new.

As I stood in the Divine Presence, Jesus first spoke to me at length about how I began to drift away from Him, and how the world was able to seduce and swallow me. He showed me a particular moment when I was a toddler. I saw myself at home at age three, surrounded by my parents, brothers, and my grandfather. Grandpa was giving me a beautiful toy, a firetruck gift-wrapped so lavishly as to impress any small child. I had to wait for what felt like eternity until the end of some kind of ceremony before I could receive my gift, which caused me great anguish.

In the heart of the giver and those adults who would witness the giving process, I saw their unconscious sense of importance and pride in bestowing such a special present. By the time I received it, the gift went from being a toy to being my first possession—an object that would cause tears if I had to share it with others, or the need to bargain and trade it for another attractive object. It is difficult to understand the gravity of such an interchange that can happen between an adult and a child. The Lord told me that this was my first step away from Him and my introduction into slavery to material things.[i]

Through His teachings, the Lord settled the question as to why I had been standing in evil territory. The Catholic Church was a blessing bestowed upon me, a product of many generations in alliance with each other, going as far back as Abraham. To have been born a Catholic was neither an accident of human destiny nor a simple decision made by my biological parents. They did not impose this on me. When I abandoned the Church at fourteen years old, I left behind the sacraments that were protecting me in this physical world. The Sacrament of Confession would have chased Satan from my soul. In my pride, I blocked God's ultimate gift to me: reception of the Eucharist, because, as Jesus taught me, we only receive Him in the Eucharist to the extent that Jesus lives in us. Highlighting the moment that I stopped receiving the Sacrament of Reconciliation, the Lord said to me, "That was your biggest loss."

The contamination that I went through in the 1960s led me to forfeiting my God-given gifts. Consequently, I was left unarmed, like unbelievers who lack specific guidance in their life's journey. My path became one of ever-increasing darkness because I had no resistance to evil forces.

Like everyone born with the blessing of Christianity, I received in Baptism the fire of the Holy Spirit. The Lord explained to me that the enemy knew my blessings only too well and sought to remove the mystical presence of the Church within me. That is why he replaced it with eastern spirituality, occultism, and all kinds of New Age practices, giving me the illusion of possessing "life in the spirit." For thirty-three years, I was the one in the parable of the talents who buried the talent. Every soul that came along in my life was to be nurtured with the goods I had buried, but instead, I fed them with tarot cards, astrology, the I-Ching, yoga, Reiki, Feng Shui, and other esoteric teachings from the east. The Lord told me, "That is not what I gave you." Each one of us, He said, is going to face God with an account of how we used His gifts. We are responsible for the talents He has given to us.

CHAPTER 2

Sin and Salvation

The Lord taught me that when we are conceived, one creature with two natures is created: the nature of the Spirit, called the soul, and the nature of the flesh, called the body. One grows up to die, and the other grows up to live forever. Sadly today, the great majority of mankind is dedicated almost exclusively to feeding the nature that is going to die. The pervasive spiritual ignorance in which humanity finds itself is such, Jesus said, that our present times are worse than those of Babylon or Sodom and Gomorrah.

Our bodies, formed from dust, carry toward heaven the treasure of the Holy Spirit in our souls, if we are faithful to God. But our bodies can also be used as trash cans of Satan, where he dumps his excrement, if we use our flesh for wrongdoing. The precious gift of our physical being then becomes our greatest nightmare—our vehicle for eternal damnation. The great calling on our lives is to save our souls. Nothing less than our eternal life is at stake.

While alive on earth, we are in a constant battle between two armies: the guardians of virtue and the guardians of vice. We cannot see them, but they are around us at every moment. Those who walk in the spiritual territory of God, while on earth, have all of heaven at their disposal and a guardian angel as their faithful guide.

The Lord showed me how heaven is made up of an ordered hierarchy, and how the army of the devil was formed when one-third of the angels fell from heaven in perfect formation,[ii] becoming a military force lined up in disobedience. He who walks in the devil's territory has a fallen angel as his guardian. Every fallen angel around him tries to make sure he goes to the wrong place, while his good guardian angel fights to save his soul until his dying breath.

The Lord showed me that sin is currently a way of life. Everything is justified so that we can live unattached to the Ten Commandments. The occult, once scorned and underground, is now mainstream. Drugs are being pushed and made legal. Violence has been industrialized. The persecution of purity has turned into a slogan of fashion. The Church is a target for comedians. Religious life is described as a model of fanaticism. Racism, vanity, pride, greed, power-seeking, fornication, homosexual acts, gay marriage, adoption by homosexual couples, in vitro fertilization, abortion, contraception, materialism, cursing the Lord's name, and so on, have been normalized.

Atheistic and New Age thought has turned entire generations of Christians into pagans within a few decades. Acting through the occult and many practices of the east, the enemy has estranged many from Christ's teachings. Satan has fooled masses by promoting the immense error of reincarnation, as just one example. Jesus liberated us from this lie. The truth is we live only once in the flesh. The soul only returns to another material body at the moment of the last judgment, at which time a perfect physical body will be given.

The intention of the evil one is to lead human beings to a primitive spiritual state, taking them back to a period three or four thousand years before Christ. Instead of preserving the grace of 2,000 years of accumulated wisdom obtained after the Resurrection of Our Lord, evil has led humanity to a state of spiritual regression.

The Lord showed me this material world, and I could see it as a very small instant in eternity. In that instant, thousands of souls were being wasted, blinded and wandering, certain that they were fighting to conquer something real and permanent. It was sad to see so many people trapped in all the techniques of "self-realization" and "personal growth" that supposedly lead them to achieve any goal in their lives with the belief that they, by their own means, are able to achieve anything they desire. This self-focused thinking, another product of atheistic science and the New Age, has deified man to the point of convincing him that he has absolute control over himself. These errors have even penetrated the Church. A dangerous mistake for us is to feed our intelligence with worldly knowledge before subjecting our minds to the divine wisdom of the Word of God.

Self-focused thinking is causing many of us to spend most of our lives passing up golden opportunities for enriching ourselves with heavenly treasures because we are too concerned with accumulating material ones, which will eventually become dilapidated, if not stolen by thieves.[iii] The Lord explained to me that everything we possess has a mouth that needs to be fed. If we have a chair, we have to find a space for it and maintain it—and so it is with each of our material possessions. If we evaluate the real stature of our spirituality, we have to look around us and assess our wealth, analyzing what we really need and taking note of what is not necessary to keep. The Lord told me that most people with possessions are smothered by them in such a way that they end up enslaved to them, when they should be giving them to the poor. There are people who reach the point of missing opportunities that might improve their lives; they cannot do things such as mobilize themselves to relocate because they cannot take all of their material possessions along. They turn their lives into an absurd irony.

Many people today are also holding onto the ridiculous belief that they are superior to others because of their race. They think that because they are white, they are better than those who are black. Many black people think they are better than whites. A lot of Asian people think they are better than the rest, and vice versa, and so on. This is a pitiful mess, a terrible delusion that the devil has planted in our hearts. If we stand before the Tribunal of God, with a lifetime of believing we were better than others because of our race, we will find ourselves in a lot of trouble. In the end, do we think that the soul has any color? Our soul has no color, and our soul is what will transcend this life.

Those in the greatest danger are lukewarm souls. It is easier for the Lord to pull a terrible sinner like me out of the devil's trash can and into the light, than to grab onto a lukewarm soul, who is more slippery than soap. When things are going badly, the lukewarm soul becomes good and behaves. Once everything is working in his favor again, he goes back to being bad, while trying to hold onto what was gained by being good. He plays a very dangerous game because he cannot tell the light from the dark.

We are lacking knowledge of the real presence of the devil in our lives. The Lord shared this with me, referring to those who should know, due to having received the grace of the Holy Spirit through Baptism. Sadly, the vast majority of Christians, over two billion, are not aware of the Gospel and do not have the grace-filled teachings of Christ in the New Testament—the perfect map of salvation in their lives. Those who have not been baptized in Christ, such as unbelievers, Jews, and Muslims, are going to be called to Divine Justice according to the gifts and graces the Lord has given them.

Anyone can provide reasons why God, purgatory,[iv] hell, or the devil do not exist, but this will not change the truth. Most assuredly, they exist, as my witness testifies—not to mention the testament of Holy Scripture. We will all be judged on how we loved God and our neighbor. The Lord explained to me that it is easier for an unbeliever with no knowledge of Christ or the Creator, who is leading a life in harmony with God, his neighbor, and himself, to find salvation than the Christian who had the appropriate tools of knowledge, doctrine, and religious practice at his disposal, and chose instead not to use them, burying them as I did.

Salvation is for everyone, the Lord said to me. God creates a human being to take him home. Because Jesus is the Judge, and all souls go through Christ to the Father, those headed for heaven turn into Christians by the time they face the Tribunal of God.[v]

Buddhists, Hindus, Muslims, atheists, Jews—all are called to salvation, but some have been given more responsibility than others. If you practice a religion that claims to be the only one that opens a door to salvation, then you have the wrong religion. The Almighty is a God of love.[4]

Yet while all are called to salvation, not many are heeding the call. This is the meaning of the Biblical phrase, "Many are called, but few are chosen."[vi] In order to acquire the Kingdom of eternal life, a soul standing before the Lord needs only the love that it gave away during its lifetime, as well as the love of suffering for a greater good. Love is the divine essence from which the soul gives and receives true nourishment.

If we never loved, we are not able to receive the love of God. When a person dies in a state of mortal sin, the first thing he does is go against himself, as I did. He starts to hate himself, to feel guilty and remorseful, and then he realizes the enemy, Satan, is his partner. He hates him, too, and at the end of all that, he ends up hating God forever—all because of pride, inordinate self-love, vanity, and pretentiousness. The Lord explained this to me by comparison with what can happen when a starving person is handed a bowl of hot soup. That person is most likely going to faint. When the light of God tries to enter the spiritually undernourished soul, the soul faints and crawls into the dark. It is not able to take the light because it never approached the light during its lifetime. This is the ultimate tragedy. We go into hell on our own. The Lord only wants to save us. And if there is anything I can testify to with

---

4 Marino Restrepo is not saying here that following Christ is not the door to salvation. It is. Much of Marino's ministry is focused on emphasizing the need and urgency of evangelizing souls. He has also been shown by Jesus that everyone in heaven is Christian, in the sense that in the presence of Truth, they believe and worship Jesus as Lord. But if someone has not been properly introduced to Christ and to the Church, through no fault of their own, they will not be condemned to hell for being a Hindu, a Buddhist, a Muslim, etc. God reaches the non-Christian where and how He can through the good that is in their beliefs in order to draw them closer to Him, and when they die, they will see Christ and have the choice to accept or reject Him.

my life. . . the mercy of God is beyond anything we can dream of or imagine.

The entrance of a soul in mortal sin before the Holy Tribunal is like the arrival of a prisoner surrounded by his jailers, and in the company of the most saddened celestial guardians, who were rejected by the soul. This is a painful march, a lost battle, the conquering of good. Only Divine Mercy can change such a terrible imprisonment of a soul in the territory of the evil one. No one from our earthly life will be with us to lend support before the Judgment Seat of God. We alone are responsible for our own behavior—good or bad. We cannot blame what was bad on our mother, father, neighbor, the president, our health, our lot in life—on anybody or anything. Our actions and our inaction will be our only witness. The Lord desires to save us from ourselves. I needed to be saved from me. I accepted Satan as a partner in my life through my own will. He came to me with a lot of proposals, but I'm the one who said yes. I was my worst enemy.

CHAPTER 3

God and Christianity

God will not judge us on the basis of the churches to which we belonged, but if we have been stiff-necked in our interactions with our brothers and sisters, He will severely punish us. Those born into Protestant churches will be judged as Protestants, since that was the gift they received from the Lord. People born into the Catholic Church who stubbornly persist in focusing on its errors and join a Protestant church will not be judged as members of the Protestant church, but as cradle Catholics who left the Church.

We are not called to convert our fellow Christians, only those who don't know the Lord or have left the fold. As Christians, we all belong to Christ; therefore, we should stay where the Lord has called us, unless God provides the Protestant with the grace of embracing the Catholic faith—in which case, it will be the gift of a greater duty and responsibility within Christianity, elevating his spirituality. There is no reason for a Protestant to lure a Catholic away from the Church. This is enough reason to see that something is very wrong. To do this is like entering the house of a married man, trying to convince him that his marriage is not good enough, and offering to find him a better spouse. This is the sad reality of many Protestants who believe their mission is to draw Catholics away from the Catholic Church. Some Catholics also feel compelled to focus on leading Protestants to Catholicism. Let us turn our separate lives in Christ into a family unit, even if we worship Him under different roofs.

CHAPTER 4
The Soul's Economy

To be aware of the administration of what the Lord called our "soul's economy" is exceedingly important in our relationship with God. To share all that the Lord taught me on this subject would take several books, but I will do my best to summarize it.

In order to receive the graces God wants to give us, we must be fully present in the moment—now. We worry to death about tomorrow, when He hasn't given it to us yet. If we do today right, tomorrow will be even better. The Lord wants us to live in the eternal present, and the enemy of our souls wants to keep us in tomorrow or yesterday. Why? Because if we are ever going to receive a grace from God, it will be in the present moment. We are not going to get today's grace tomorrow, and we certainly didn't receive it yesterday. Every day, we rush past many graces that God extends to us. We have to be present and alert in Christ, where we are. "Be alert!" says the Gospel in so many ways.[vii] The Lord told me that we forget His teaching that we need to prepare ourselves to see Him today, not tomorrow. We fall asleep because the devil has tricked us into believing that eternal life only begins when we die.

All of us are standing in eternity right now. All of the actions and prayers of our lives, from childhood to our death, permanently endure in eternity. We will review them all during our personal judgment, when we come before the Divine Presence. Only when we establish harmony with heaven, and we restore all the moments that we lived disconnected from the spirit, can we stand in the Presence of God, gloriously free.

Every instant of our life, whether we are engaged in goodness or evil, is present in eternity. That is why our acts are clearly marked on one side or the other. Our relationship with the forces of good and evil are the determining factor of our "account" before the Lord. Therefore, we must keep strict vigilance over our actions and prayer life so that the "numbers" will not multiply in the wrong territory, invariably exposing our souls to grave danger of damnation. Our inaction and all of our actions have repercussions that extend far beyond us, including those things we do in secret. Our account is very large. That is why we have to work on the "numbers" before it is too late. Just as our hairs are counted[viii] and our days are numbered,[ix] so are our deeds.[x] When we die, our account comes up immediately. We will see how we are the result of what we did with sin and with grace.

I call it "the account" only to be able to illustrate in a practical and rational way that there is not a single moment of our lives that will escape the eyes of Jesus — or of ourselves. Interpenetrated by the Lord, I was made perfectly aware of my entire earthly life in the territory of good and evil. Yet the redemption we have been given by God the Father through His Son, Jesus Christ, is so large that through His merits, we are capable of paying every single debt against us with His blood.[xi] It is possible, then, while we are still living in the flesh, not only to pay off all of our existing debts, but also to repay the consequences inflicted by them.

In the Gospels, Christ exhorts us to be perfect as His Heavenly Father is perfect. He shows us the path, the way, the truth. He promises us eternal life, but also warns us that it is better to resolve our accounts with our opponents in this life because if we do not do so, we will be taken to jail and unable to leave until we have paid the very last cent. I do not think that there is a better example or a clearer description of purgatory than this gospel parable given by Our Lord.[xii] We are in the flesh, and everything we have damaged through sin has to be repaired in this body, otherwise once we leave this earth, we can no longer repair anything. If we are destined for heaven, we have to be purged, and purgation is a very painful state.

A parallel understanding of the pain of purgatory would be when a relative dies with whom we had unfinished business, and we are not at peace. That person is gone, and in our heart remains a great void of loneliness and regret over that particular relationship. Similarly, one of the greatest pains of a soul once undressed from the flesh is to discover all of its wasted graces. After death, no more graces are allowed. One must then live the time of justice and go through a painful purgatory, where souls are not at peace with themselves and long for the light that they have to gain back. They feel joy in knowing their salvation is assured, but at the same time, they experience a great sadness because they are still tied to what happened in this world, witnessing all their unloving acts, or their lack of loving action. The Lord told me that we have forgotten a basic reality: we can only enter heaven directly if we are saints. And it is better to become a saint on earth through our own will than to become a saint in purgatory against our will.

Christians are the Church Militant on earth, the souls in purgatory are the Church Suffering, and the saints in heaven are the Church Triumphant. A soul in purgatory cannot pray for himself, but he can pray for those on earth. A soul on earth can pray for himself and for souls in purgatory, and saints in heaven can pray for all. The Lord showed me that when a soul in the flesh prays for a soul in purgatory, they align together, as both look to God for mercy and compassion. If the soul in purgatory is suffering due to the sin of being cruel to his parents or irreverent in Church, for example, then the person on earth is able to offer a prayer of reparation on behalf of that soul to repair what he did. As a result, both souls move closer to God. That is how the prayer is answered.

The Lord told me that in regard to the soul's economy, the world is dropping the graces He is sending, therefore those who are walking in the light are receiving what is being turned down. He said that when all the members of a family are living in the dark, and one of them comes back to God, that person receives all of the graces being rejected by the rest. That person therefore is given great help to become the lantern, the shining light of the family, because to convert his loved ones and help change the world, he must become a saint.

Our loving actions performed while on earth are the most powerful sources of light. To illustrate this, the Lord showed me a certain loving act of mine while I was attending elementary school at age eight. During recess, I saw myself sitting on a wooden bench on the main patio of the school, beside a child who was physically deformed. Many of the children were making fun of him when the Lord inspired me to embrace and protect this helpless, abused child. By the grace of God, I became his protector during breaks between classes. During my personal judgment, even though I was in the enemy's territory, I witnessed Divine Justice acting in my favor.

During the time the Lord was showing me my embrace of that child, my sins that were appearing before Him were not being taken into account. My acts of love toward this child seemed to turn into a single good deed before the Holy Tribunal, representing a grace that was erasing territorial sin by leaps and bounds. As every single wrong approached the Judgment Seat of God, I watched it disappear in the presence of the Lord. If I could describe this in human terms, I would say that love and charity is the currency of heaven. Truly, charity does cover a multitude of sins.[xiii]

During my mystical experience, I was shown different scenes from my childhood. The Blessed Mother spoke to me of how I had received and shared great blessings as a child. I saw myself during Holy Week in my home town, playing my trumpet during Good Friday processions. Then I witnessed myself staying with a very sick relative at age seven, and many other moments when my brothers and sisters and I were still innocent and enveloped in beautiful light.

When we exercise charity with a humble heart, we are able to unite with an entire army of angels. When we act charitably toward someone, our guardian angel immediately joins with theirs, and they unite with us to form part of our defense and unconditional help. A person who loves his neighbor is filled with celestial inspirations. Charity, forgiveness, compassion, patience, temperance — all the virtues, are the deposits that protect us from bankruptcy of the spirit and build up our eternal wealth in the celestial bank.

If we have suffered abuse from others and yet remained loving and forgiving, our celestial bank fills quickly. This does not mean that we should allow ourselves to be abused; if we can change an abusive situation, we must do so. It means that when we live the Lord's prayer: "Forgive us our sins, as we forgive those who sin against us," we receive an abundance of grace that can advance us rapidly toward heaven, such as in the case of a mistreated schoolmate I nicknamed "gallo" (rooster), or a servant girl I verbally accosted. In the face of pain or disappointment, if we say to the Lord, "I forgive this person," or "I accept this cross of pain I cannot change — this disability, this difficult family, this job I must do," and so on — we can even be the one to break a curse of generations within our family.

CHAPTER 5
The Eucharist

The biggest act of mercy ever given to humanity is the Eucharist. Nothing compares. If it weren't for the Eucharist, our entire planet would have been annihilated already by Satan. God showed me His mystical presence during the Mass, which is so enormous that if we could but see one tiny glimpse of this mystery, we would walk into the church on our knees. Every single pew in a Catholic church, every single fount of holy water, is guarded by angels. The altar, the walls outside, every column, statue—everything is guarded against the enemy. And yet, Satan can still walk into a church. He enters attached to a prisoner in chains, as his fallen escort and guardian. This is his only way in.

The Lord also showed me how Satan, having infiltrated the Church through those who are in sin, is creating the most incredible state of confusion and spiritual disarray for the weak and lukewarm in the faith, who have not firmly decided on which of the two spiritual territories they reside. The lukewarm parishioner is easy prey for the devil. He easily believes those who are spreading erroneous teachings, and during Mass, he is distracted by this person's dress, that person's cough, and another's way of walking. He is taken elsewhere by his own thoughts because he is not there visiting the Lord; he is visiting his little, mischievous ways.

We cannot anchor our faith in the humanness of the Church. It is important to understand that when we enter a Catholic church, the Lord, Himself, is there to greet us. If we could only visualize the spiritual nourishment we receive from the Church. If we could only fathom the beauty of the spiritual life in the Church during the celebration of the Eucharist, or a visit to the Blessed Sacrament, while praying the Stations of the Cross, or during any devotion, especially the Rosary, we would enter the Church with great joy.

Every time we take Communion, we can help rescue souls. At that very moment, the Lord makes us Christlike, according to the degree that we've made room for Him in our hearts. Through the Eucharist, our body becomes like Christ's Body, our blood turns into Christ's Blood, and with it, the Lord is able to rescue a soul that otherwise would have been condemned.

We are told by St. Luke in the Book of Acts that after Pentecost, the apostles had no fear and would preach in the temple, where the enemies of Jesus congregated. Before preaching, the apostles would bless and break the bread at home (celebrating the Eucharist).[xiv] Knowing that the apostles would walk by on their way to the temple, people would line up the sick and the possessed on the sidewalks. Scripture speaks of how Peter's shadow passing by would heal and deliver them.[xv] Why? He was carrying this power of the Lord's Body and Blood within him.

Angels and saints, who exist in the eternal present and are not confined to time and space, can see the light that we are holding and radiating. It is not a light that can be seen by us, for it would be blinding, like the light radiating from Moses' face after he spoke to God on Mt. Sinai. The Hebrews couldn't bear to look his way so they covered his face with a veil in order to talk to him. After we receive Communion, wherever we go, wonders are taking place. People are being healed. People are being delivered. The same kinds of miracles happen when we have spent time in Adoration of the Blessed Sacrament. We will know about this economy on the day we appear before the Holy Tribunal of the Lord. Until then, we won't even notice them. In this hidden way, the Lord keeps us humble and small, protecting us from spiritual pride, which is Satan.

Jesus told me He had gifted me with the greatest responsibility that can be given to a human being. It was to be a Eucharistic instrument of reparation. That is what being a Catholic means. This doesn't mean that Catholics are better than anyone else. Nor does it mean that they are the only ones who will make it to heaven. Every time a person takes Communion in a state of grace, he not only nourishes his own soul, but also feeds souls around the world — such is the power of receiving God. Those who are Catholic are therefore responsible for all souls of humanity, regardless of where those souls are and what they are about. Catholics are responsible because of the Eucharist. Having such power at their disposal, they must use it, especially because no one besides those who have the Eucharist can.

CHAPTER 6

Baptism

The Lord also spoke to me about the Sacrament of Baptism. He explained that the soul begins its accounting at the moment of conception. When God creates a human being, the calculations commence and are added to the total sum of the spiritual economy of his or her biological family. This is called intergenerational inheritance. A person can receive millions of blessings as a consequence of the good actions of his ancestors. A person can also receive curses that are for a limited number of generations. If one's biological mother is not in God's grace and has inherited intergenerational debt from her ancestors—in other words, is under the yoke of original sin—her baby will begin a difficult journey, facing adversity every step of the way. The sin the child will encounter will conflict with his spiritual expectations of goodness, which exist because of his soul's inherent state of grace before leaving the mother's womb and entering sinful territory.

Baptism frees the creature from all intergenerational debt, and the soul's economy enters a field of grace, where the Divine Judge opens a brand-new account. After Baptism, every soul has unlimited spiritual potential. The soul is like a treasure chest filled with jewels of goodness, which if protected, will lead to spiritual enrichment and harmony with the material world. A soul whose spiritual economy is no longer tied to intergenerational debt and attachments is an anointed being, blessed by the Holy Spirit.

The Lord showed me how many of the sins that affect our lives from our early years are consequences of the acts of our ancestors.

He also said that if we are baptized and then commit a mortal sin, the freedom that we gained through Baptism is lost, and we again receive the afflictions of our ancestors. Our spiritual economy then hangs in the balance.

CHAPTER 7

The Sacrament of Reconciliation

The Lord shared how He came to earth in bodily form to repair the damage in the flesh due to sin—past, present, and future. He left us with a sacred instrument in the flesh: the priest. With the ordination of the priesthood, these men are able to free us from sin and the chains that bind us to the devil.

One of the most clever tricks of Satan is to make Catholics believe that confessing our sins directly to Jesus will suffice, and that there is no need of a middleman. If that were the case, what would have been the role of the twelve Apostles chosen by Jesus to go out and proclaim the Good News of salvation? The Lord could have done this without the Apostles—the middlemen. When the Lord paired His disciples and sent them out, He chose to give them the power to forgive or retain sins, telling them,

> "Peace be with you. As the Father has sent me, so I send you." And when he had said this, he breathed on them and said to them, "Receive the Holy Spirit. Whose sins you forgive are forgiven them, and whose sins you retain are retained."[xvi]

How could one dispute this command by Jesus? The Sacrament of Confession was established at that time. This Sacrament turns the priest into a spiritual vessel of the Holy Spirit. The Lord explained to me that when we are with the priest in the confessional, we should pray to the Holy Spirit so that the priest's physical presence disappears and is replaced by the Holy Spirit during Confession.

The power of Confession is tremendous and often underestimated. Used to its full potential, it guides us into releasing one of the heaviest burdens that we carry — the burden of sin. When we confess our sins, we arrest all the activities of the devil in our lives. In effect, we take him captive before the Holy Spirit and hand him over with his entire army to the Confessional, where he belongs. No demon can handle the Sacrament of Reconciliation.

If we haven't confessed for years and our hearts are repentant, the Holy Spirit will, at long last, release us from the grip of the evil one. Should we die after making a sincere confession, we will stand before the Holy Tribunal of the Lord in the territory of goodness. This does not mean that we will automatically go straight to heaven; we still must make reparation for our sins. (See Council of Trent.[xvii])

Why was I built up with so much pride and a slave to the flesh? Because I was not absolved through the Sacrament of Reconciliation. The Lord showed me how I took away my own spiritual protection and left myself chained to the army of the devil, the guardians of my sins — for every single sin that has not been confessed and atoned for is guarded by demons.

It is a great act of humility to kneel down and confess one's sins to a man, and the devil hates humility. Some people look for the most holy priest to confess to, but kneeling to confess our sins before a priest who is bad spiritual shape infuriates Satan even more, because doing so is a most humbling act. Regardless of the state of the priest's soul, the Sacrament frees us from our chains, and like in an exorcism, Satan and his army are sent off to prison. This is the great miracle of Confession that the Lord left behind for us.

When we are unchained from sin, we are left with the wounds of sin, like skin that has been damaged from being bound for a long time. The devil will breathe through these wounds. Our sins may haunt us still, if we receive God's forgiveness but will not forgive ourselves. The greatest healing balm for the soul is the Eucharist. It renews and rebuilds what was hurt in the soul because of sin, and fills the space within us that was occupied by the devil. Through the Eucharist, the Lord leads us to love, to the gifts of the Spirit, to sainthood.

Feeding our soul with the Eucharist is also an act of reparation. Since Jesus Christ became flesh in order to repair in His flesh the damage due to sin, what better flesh is there for this purpose than the Body and Blood of Jesus Christ in the Holy Eucharist? Our invisible soul is healed by the invisible mystery of the Transubstantiation: the great miracle of Jesus turning simple bread and wine into His very own Body and Blood—for us. After Confession, which is the cleansing of our spiritual house, our soul should immediately be occupied by the Lord so that the enemy cannot take up residence through a spiritual vacuum. If we take Communion and truly believe that Jesus dwells in the Eucharist, then our act of reparation will be consummated, leading us to make atonement for our sins. However, not fully believing in the Real Presence will make our act of reparation imperfect. If we happen to die and come before the Lord at that moment, our souls will still be stained with sin, due to our disbelief.

One of the best ways of repairing ourselves after being forgiven is to try not to sin again. Nonetheless, when it inevitably happens, we must immediately go to the Sacrament of Reconciliation and repent, before sin begins to destroy our souls again. If we stay in mortal sin longer than a day, we will fall into the excrement pit of the devil and end up in a worse condition than before we last went to Confession, because the devil strikes more ferociously at those who have fallen from grace.

CHAPTER 8

Conversion

When a person undergoes a conversion after receiving the grace to discover sin and find God, he is not aware of the darkness that still accompanies him. Even when the soul makes a firm decision to divorce the devil, the devil will still relentlessly try to ensnare him until his last breath. Consequently, reflection and spiritual direction, in the strictest form, are required because the legion that kept him company over the years is not going to let go of him easily. It is a case of extreme seriousness, and we have to make the converted soul aware that severing his relationship with Satan is warfare that will demand all of his attention.

If we have strayed from the true path and returned to the light, we can see the tracks that were left behind in the enemy's territory. It is costly to clean our soul and recover our innocence and angelic company. We are all called to present ourselves, just as we are, at the foot of our crucified Lord. This means bringing Him everything so that He can receive, purify, and repair any damage, in order to free us.

We should come before Him with our past and place it before the foot of the cross of Jesus, asking him to cover any darkness with His Blood, so that it may never again be counted against us before His Holy Tribunal. We should come before Him with our afflictions and say: "Lord, at Your crucified feet, I come to prostrate myself, to give you this pain, suffering, anguish, trial, disease. . . I want you, Lord, to receive it so that You can make it Your will. I know that

You did not send me this particular trial, but I also know that You taught us the way of Calvary. You call us to carry our own cross and to unite it with Yours. Make of my pain whatever You will. Let this contribute to the salvation of my soul, to the souls of my family, and to whatever intentions You have, as You receive this. And if You want to heal me, save me from this trial . . . this disease . . . this pain. Glory to you, Almighty Lord."

God does not test anyone. We bring trials and tribulations upon ourselves because of our sins, and the prosecutor of any test is Satan, the source and fountain of all sin. The discipline or mortification of our lower nature has a purifying effect on our flesh, turning it into the temple of the Holy Spirit.

Because of the evil one, we were born in a very painful way through the fall of Adam and Eve, and we will die through physical deterioration. Through original sin, we have all entered into a relationship with the enemy. We have to assume this reality in concrete terms; otherwise, we will never understand our weaknesses, misery, fragility, vulnerability, and the evil that is in us because of our lineage. Understanding our fallen nature leads us into union with the Spirit.

If we have no love for our flesh, the world can offer us nothing. The evil one will have no way of perverting us if we are detached from our physical self. The flesh turns into our worst enemy if we do not recognize our sinful nature. Armed with this knowledge, we can begin training our physical bodies in the same way that a horse is tamed. The spirit is the rider, and the body is the horse. When we know the nature of this animal, we are able to have it under our control and discipline. A horse with a rider is a useful element of labor, a vehicle that facilitates the execution of innumerable duties. When we subject the flesh to strict obedience of the Holy Spirit, He will be the one riding our instrument. The Lord will dwell within us, and we within Him.

CHAPTER 9
Spiritual Growth & Maintenance

Spiritual growth and maintenance is difficult to master and the most important battle to conquer. Our souls depend on it so that our sins do not accumulate and turn into currents of darkness that may break loose and get out of control. The angels of God constantly invite us to an inner cleansing through Confession, fasting, penance, and mortification. These weapons help us to maintain the purity of our souls, which are unceasingly bombarded by Satan's tempting proposals.

The devil doesn't like to leave us alone. Wearing blessed objects helps to protect us from his antics. If we wear a crucifix, demons see the real crucified Christ; if we wear the Miraculous Medal, demons see the Virgin Mary; and this disarms them. But even when we go to Mass, Satan is there. We can be sitting in a pew, concentrating on the proclamation of God's Word, then wake up to the realization that the Gospel was already read, and we didn't hear it. The enemy stole the moment and took us somewhere else. He knows how important it is for us to hear the Word because that same Word proclaimed at Mass is about to become God's flesh. How much of Jesus we receive when we go to Communion depends upon how much of His Life and Word are already within us.

Even if we are doing well spiritually, Satan will sneak in by trying to shorten our lifespan or make us ill through something we are doing—perhaps a developing addiction, a relationship, over-working, bad eating or drinking habits, or through something that appears, at face value, to be very good.

St. Paul spoke of the flaming arrows of the evil one.[xviii] When the devil shoots arrows at us, it is because he is far away. If he is close, he will be stabbing us. Burning arrows are therefore a grace, but we have to be alert because we are being shot at all the time. Yet the Christian can turn every arrow into a grace. The human being living in God's territory is offered a sure solution to every human dilemma that presents itself, and even the smallest soldier of Christ can defeat the greatest army of the devil.

To defeat the enemy means to open our arms wide with love, to lay down on the wood of the cross and let our persecutors humiliate us, nail us, stab us in the side, and crown us with thorns. The Lord asked me, "Who are you to be offended? You are only clay." The opposite of the cross is to curl ourselves into a defensive position of self-protection and say, "I've been betrayed. I can't trust anymore." We are called to open up and to follow a path of pain and suffering. The gate is very narrow, and the way of the cross is bloody and thorny. People do not want to accept such suffering as healing.

The Lord provides the strength necessary to overcome our sin with divine perfection. He has done so with the saints, allowing them to go through great temporal torments in order to purify their fallen nature. He knows how transitory our suffering is and how terrible it is to be purified after our earthly life. The mercy of God is immeasurable. It has no borders or preferences; God loves His creatures.

To be surrounded by God's angels and saints, all we have to do is stand beside a humble human being. Since everything exists at the same time in the spiritual plateau—heaven, purgatory, hell, and this earthly life—the one who is humble is walking in heaven already. The Lord demonstrates in every possible way that the only path to salvation is sanctity; therefore, let us not expect that accepting Jesus as our Savior, reading Scripture, and proclaiming Him everywhere is enough to obtain perfection and reparation for our sins. We must also humbly embrace the cross with acts of authentic sacrifice and legitimate charity, obeying the Ten Commandments and the Church's teachings, and living each day in God's will. By doing so, we display our humility and loyalty to God; and in the process, we become more like Him.

We are called to carry the silence of the cross by offering our pain, trials, and tribulations to the Lord, instead of giving them away to others. Whenever we share our cross with our neighbor, not only do we waste spiritual treasures of merit and true healing, but we accumulate darkness for our souls because of the lack of charity and respect for our neighbor. The silence of the cross invites us into the true silence of the spirit, which is the gift of inner peace in the midst of this painful world.

Only in God will we be able to face the absurd misery that is part of our human existence. With His support, we will transcend to the divine and find meaning, even in our suffering and pain. I can testify to His infinite love—a love that would calcify our existence if we were to receive it all at once. That is why He dispenses His love to us little by little, like the sun, which gives us life and sight and warmth through its rays, without burning us in its incandescent fire. That love is our very life. The only thing we can retain from our earthly existence is the love from His rays that we give away.

The human being living in God's territory is offered a sure solution to every human dilemma that presents itself. The longer a person continues to be in the state of grace, the greater light that he assimilates because his company of angels and saints ever increases, turning him into a true fountain of goodness and possibility. If he fights continuously to maintain the light of the Holy Spirit, it will shine like a lamp over every step of his journey. At the same time, he opens up an accessible path to everyone around him, generating a sea of light in union with Light itself, which is radiated by the great numbers of heavenly hosts who surround him.

The entrance of a soul in the state of grace before the Tribunal of the Lord is like the triumphal entrance of a soldier returning from war, escorted by a great army of warriors who kept him company during battle. It is the triumph of the soul, the day of crowning for the Christian. Through the legacy of prayer and good works left behind on earth, he continues from heaven the battle for souls, until the day of Jesus Christ's final return.

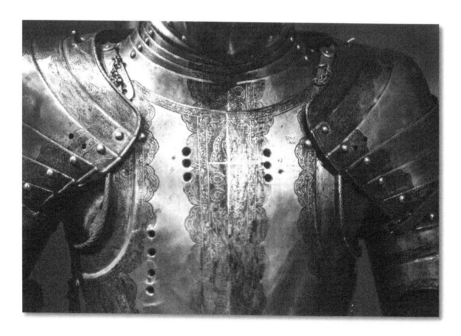

NOTES TO THE READER

Amazon Reviews

If you were graced by this book, would you kindly post a short review of *Winning the Battle for Your Soul* on Amazon.com? Your support will make a difference in the lives of souls and our future.

To leave a short review, go to Amazon.com and type in *Winning the Battle for Your Soul*. Click on the book and scroll down the page. Next to customer reviews, click on "Write a customer review." Thank you, in advance, for your kindness.

Marino Restrepo's Full Story

The story of Marino Restrepo with the details of his kidnapping, his illumination of conscience, his experience of being before the Judgment Seat, his encounter with Jesus and Mary, and more, can be read in the #1 Amazon best-seller, *The Warning: Testimonies and Prophecies of the Illumination of Conscience*.

More information to help you
Find Your Way Home

Sign up for the Queen of Peace Media monthly newsletter to be informed of resources to help you navigate these tumultuous times.

www.QueenofPeaceMedia.com/newsletter

More Messages from Heaven

See the following website for the most up-to-date, reliable, and comprehensive source on the Internet of private revelation concerning our tumultuous times:

www.CountdowntotheKingdom.com.

OTHER BOOKS
by the author

Available through
QueenofPeaceMedia.com and Amazon.com
in Print, Ebook, and Audiobook formats

Libros disponible en español
www.queenofpeacemedia.com/libreria-catolica

EL AVISO
Testimonios y Profecías de la Iluminación de Conciencia

EL MANTO DE MARÍA
Una Consagración Mariana para Ayuda Celestial

EL MANTO DE MARÍA
Diario de Oración para la Consagración

TRANSFIGURADA
La Historia de Patricia Sandoval

HOMBRES JUNTO A MARÍA
Así Vencieron Seis Hombres la Más Ardua Batalla
de Sus Vidas

THE WARNING

TESTIMONIES AND PROPHECIES OF THE ILLUMINATION OF CONSCIENCE
with *IMPRIMATUR*

en español:
EL AVISO

Endorsed by Bishop Gavin Ashenden, Msgr. Ralph J. Chieffo, Fr. John Struzzo, Mark Mallet, Fr. Berdardin Mugabo, and more...

Includes the fascinating story of Marino Restrepo, hailed as a St. Paul for our century

(See www.queenofpeacemedia.com/the-warning for the book trailer)

The Warning has been an Amazon #1 best-seller, ever since its release. In the book are authentic accounts of saints and mystics of the Church who have spoken of a day when we will all see our souls in the light of truth, and fascinating stories of those who have already experienced it for themselves.

"With His divine love, He will open the doors of hearts and illuminate all consciences. Every person will see himself in the burning fire of divine truth. It will be like a judgment in miniature."
—**Our Lady to Fr. Stefano Gobbi of the Marian Movement of Priests**

SHE WHO SHOWS THE WAY

HEAVEN'S MESSAGES
FOR OUR TURBULENT TIMES

"This book should be widely disseminated, all for God's glory and in honor of the Mother of God, for all of us and the holiness of Christ's disciples."
— **Ramón C. Argüelles, STL, Archbishop-Emeritus**

(See www.QueenofPeaceMedia.com and Amazon.com)

Our Mother knows when we most need her, and we need her now.

We are living in the end times, not the end of the world, but the end of an age. Those who wish to remain faithful to the Gospel are seeking heaven's guidance in order to weather and safely navigate the unparalleled storms ahead.

In this extraordinary and anointed book of messages from Mother Mary—and occasionally from Jesus—through authentic inner-locutions to one of her most unlikely children, she has responded.

"A great turning point in the fate of your nation and its faith in God will soon be upon you, and I ask you all to pray and offer your sufferings for this cause. . ."
— **Our Lady's message of August 4, 1993**

OF MEN AND MARY

HOW SIX MEN WON THE GREATEST BATTLE OF THEIR LIVES

"Of Men and Mary is superb. The six life testimonies contained within it are miraculous, heroic, and truly inspiring."

—**Fr. Gary Thomas**
Pastor, exorcist, and subject of the book and movie, "The Rite."

"Anointed!"
—**Fr. Donald Calloway, MIC**
(See <u>www.queenofpeacemedia.com/of-men-and-mary</u>
For the book trailer and to order)

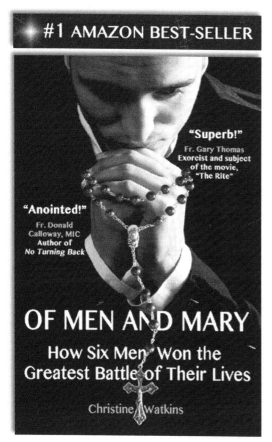

#1 AMAZON BEST-SELLER

"Superb!"
Fr. Gary Thomas
Exorcist and subject
of the movie,
"The Rite"

"Anointed!"
Fr. Donald
Calloway, MIC
Author of
No Turning Back

OF MEN AND MARY
How Six Men Won the
Greatest Battle of Their Lives

Christine Watkins

Turn these pages, and you will find yourself surprisingly inspired by a murderer locked up in prison, a drug-using football player who dreamed of the pros, and a selfish, womanizing dare-devil who died and met God. You will root for a husband and father whose marriage was a battleground, a man searching desperately to belong, pulled by lust and illicit attractions, and an innocent lamb who lost, in a single moment, everyone he cared about most. And you will rejoice that their sins and their pasts were no obstacle for heaven.

FULL OF GRACE

MIRACULOUS STORIES OF HEALING AND CONVERSION THROUGH MARY'S INTERCESSION

"Christine Watkins's beautiful and touching collection of conversion stories are direct, honest, heart-rending, and miraculous."

—Wayne Weible
Author of Medjugorje: The Message

(See www.queenofpeacemedia.com/full-of-grace for the book trailer and to order)

In this riveting book, Christine Watkins tells her dramatic story of miraculous healing and conversion to Catholicism, along with the stories of five others: a homeless drug addict, an altar boy trapped by cocaine, a stripper, a lonely youth, and a modern-day hero. Following each story is a message that Mary has given to the world.

And for those eager to probe the deeper, reflective waters of discipleship—either alone or within a prayer group—a Scripture passage, prayerful reflection questions, and a spiritual exercise at the end of each chapter offer an opportunity to enliven our faith.

TRANSFIGURED

PATRICIA SANDOVAL'S STORY

Endorsed by
**Archbishop Salvatore Cordileone & Bishop Michael Barber, SJ,
and Fr. Donald Calloway, MIC**

**Disponible También en Español: TRANSFIGURADA
avalado por EMMANUEL**

**(See www.queenofpeacemedia.com/transfigured
for the book trailer, the companion DVD, and to order)**

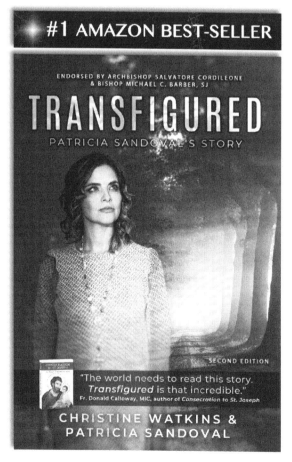

"Are you ready to read one of the most powerful conversion stories ever written? Seriously, are you? It's a bold and shocking claim, I admit. But the story you are about to have the pleasure of reading is so intense and brutally candid that I wouldn't be surprised if it brings you to tears multiple times and opens the door to an experience of mercy and healing. This story is made for the big screen, and I pray it makes it there someday. It's that incredible. . . What you are about to read is as raw, real, and riveting as a story can get. I couldn't put this book down!"

—**Fr. Donald Calloway,
MIC**
Author of
Consecration to St. Joseph
and *No Turning Back*

MARY'S MANTLE CONSECRATION

A SPIRITUAL RETREAT FOR HEAVEN'S HELP

Disponible también en español—*El Manto de María: Una Consagración Mariana para Ayuda Celestial*

Endorsed by **Archbishop Salvatore Cordileone** and **Bishop Myron J. Cotta**

(See www.MarysMantleConsecration.com to see a video of amazing testimonies and to order)

"I am grateful to Christine Watkins for making this disarmingly simple practice, which first grew in the fertile soil of Mexican piety, available to the English-speaking world."
—**Archbishop Salvatore Cordileone**

"Now more than ever, we need a miracle. Christine Watkins leads us through a 46-day self-guided retreat that focuses on daily praying of the Rosary, a Little fasting, and meditating on various virtues and the seven gifts of the Holy Spirit, leading to a transformation in our lives and in the people on the journey with us!"
—**Fr. Sean O. Sheridan, TOR**
Former President, Franciscan University of Steubenville

MARY'S MANTLE CONSECRATION

PRAYER JOURNAL
to accompany the consecration book

Disponible también en español—
El Manto de Maria: Diario de Oración para la Consagración

PREPARE FOR AN OUTPOURING OF GRACE UPON YOUR LIFE

(See www.MarysMantleConsecration.com
to see a video of amazing testimonies and to order)

St. Pope John Paul II said that his consecration to Mary was "a decisive turning point in my life." It can be the same for you.

This *Prayer Journal* with daily Scriptures, saint quotes, questions for reflection and space for journaling is a companion book to the popular *Mary's Mantle Consecration*, a self-guided retreat that has resulted in miracles in the lives and hearts of those who have applied themselves to it. This prayer journal will take you even deeper into your soul and into God's transforming grace.

IN LOVE WITH TRUE LOVE

THE UNFORGETTABLE STORY OF SISTER NICOLINA

(See www.QueenofPeaceMedia.com and Amazon.com)

In this seemingly loveless world of ours, we might wonder if true love is attainable. Is it real, or is it perhaps a dancing illusion captured on Hollywood screens? And if this love dares to exist, does it satisfy as the poets say, or fade in our hearing like a passing whisper?

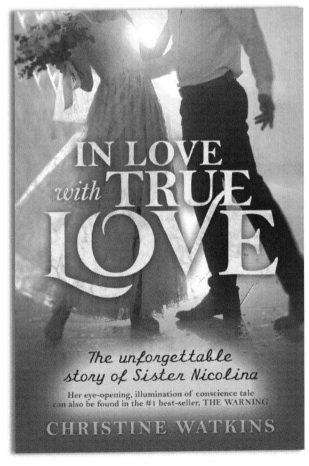

The souls are few who have discovered these answers, and one of them is Nicolina, a feisty, flirtatious girl who fell in love with the most romantic man in all of post-war Germany.

Little did they imagine the places where love would take them.

This enthralling, real-life short story is a glimpse into the grand secrets of true love—secrets that remain a conundrum to most, but become life itself for a grateful few. These hidden treasures wait in hope to be discovered, resting in chambers of the Heart of Love. Through this little book, may you, like Nicolina, enter their mystery, and find life, too.

MARIE-JULIE JAHENNY

PROPHECIES AND PROTECTION
FOR THE END TIMES

(See www.QueenofPeaceMedia.com. Soon on Amazon.com)

Marie-Julie Jahenny (1850-1941) is one of the most extraordinary mystics in the history of the Church. This humble peasant from devout parents in Britanny, France, received numerous visitations from heaven and lived with multiple wounds of the stigmata for most of her long life.

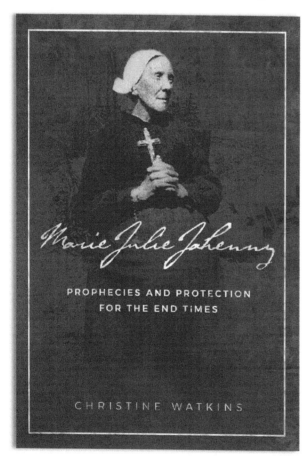

Jahenny's selfless spirit endures as a gift to the Church, for she received knowledge of what lies on the horizon of our current era.

Jahenny was supported by her local bishop, Msgr. Fournier of Nantes, who said of her, "I see nothing but good."

In addition to Jahenny's special mission from the Lord to spread the love of the Cross, she was called to prepare the world for the coming chastisements, which precede and prepare the world for the glorious renewal of Christendom in the promised era of peace.

Through Marie-Julie, the Lord has given help, remedies, and protection for the times we now live in, and those soon to come. As Christ said to her on several occasions, "I want My people to be warned."

PURPLE SCAPULAR

OF BLESSING AND PROTECTION
FOR THE END TIMES

Jesus and Mary have given this scapular to the world for our times!

Go to **www.queenofpeacemedia.com/product/purple-scapular-of-blessing-and-protection** to read about all of the incredible promises given to those who wear it in faith.

Our Lady's words to the mystic, stigmatist, and victim soul, Marie-Julie Jahenny: "My children, all souls, all people who possesses this scapular will see their family protected. Their home will also be protected, **foremost from fires**. . . for a long time my Son and I have had the desire to make known this scapular of benediction…

This first apparition of this scapular will be a new protection for the times of the chastisements, of the calamities, and the famines. All those who are clothed (with it) shall pass under the storms, the tempests, and the darkness. They will have light as if it were plain day. Such is the power of this unknown scapular…"

THE CROSS OF FORGIVENESS

FOR THE END TIMES

On July 20, 1882, Our Lord introduced THE CROSS OF FORGIVENESS to the world through the French mystic, Marie-Julie Jahenny. He indicated that He would like it made and worn by the faithful during the time of the chastisements. It is a cross signifying pardon, salvation, protection, and the calming of plagues.

Go to **www.queenofpeacemedia.com/product/cross-of-forgiveness** to read about all of the graces and protection given to those who wear it in faith.

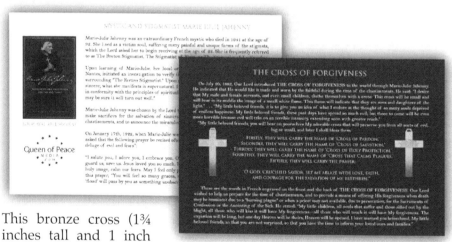

This bronze cross (1¾ inches tall and 1 inch wide) is a gift for our age and a future time when priests may not be readily available: "My little beloved friends, you will bear on yourselves My adorable cross that will preserve you from all sorts of evil, big or small, and later I shall bless them. . . My little children, all souls that suffer, and those sifted out by the blight, all those who will kiss it will have My forgiveness—all those who will touch it will have My forgiveness." The expiation will be long, but one day Heaven will be theirs, Heaven will be opened."

THE FLAME OF LOVE

THE SPIRITUAL DIARY
OF ELIZABETH KINDELMANN

(See www.QueenofPeaceMedia.com/flame-love-love-book-bundle)

Extraordinary graces of literally blinding Satan, and reaching heaven quickly are attached to the spiritual practices and promises in this spiritual classic. On August 2, 1962, Our Lady said these remarkable words to mystic and victim soul, Elizabeth Kindelmann:

"Since the Word became Flesh, I have never given such a great movement as the Flame of Love that comes to you now. Until now, there has been nothing that so blinds Satan."

THE FLAME OF LOVE

In this special talk, Christine Watkins introduces the Flame of Love of the Immaculate Heart of Mary.

This worldwide movement in the Catholic Church is making true disciples of Jesus Christ in our turbulent times and preparing souls for the Triumph of Our Lady's Heart and the New Pentecost.

See www.ChristineWatkins.com.
Email cwatkins@queenofpeacemedia.com.

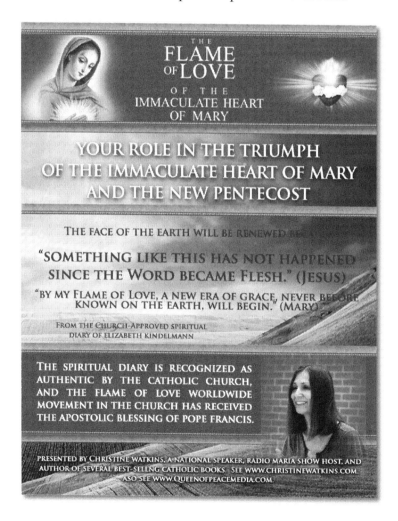

END NOTES

[i] Matthew 6:19-21

[ii] Revelation 12:7-12

[iii] Matthew 6:19-21

[iv] EXAMPLES OF PURGATORY IS IN THE BIBLE: "Then the master called the servant in. 'You wicked servant,' he said, 'I canceled all that debt of yours because you begged me to. Shouldn't you have had mercy on your fellow servant just as I had on you?' In anger his master handed him over to the jailers to be tortured, until he should pay back all he owed. "This is how my heavenly Father will treat each of you unless you forgive your brother or sister from your heart." --Matt. 18:32-35

"Settle matters quickly with your adversary who is taking you to court. Do it while you are still together on the way, or your adversary may hand you over to the judge, and the judge may hand you over to the officer, and you may be thrown into prison. Truly I tell you, you will not get out until you have paid the last penny."--Matt. 5:25

"But each one should build with care. For no one can lay any foundation other than the one already laid, which is Jesus Christ. If anyone builds on this foundation using gold, silver, costly stones, wood, hay or straw, their work will be shown for what it is, because the Day will bring it to light. It will be revealed with fire, and the fire will test the quality of each person's work. If what has been built survives, the builder will receive a reward. 15 If it is burned up, the builder will suffer loss but yet will be saved—even though ONLY as one ESCAPING THROUGH THE FLAMES. 1 Cor. 3:11-15

Matt. 5:26,18:34; Luke 12:58-59 -- Jesus teaches us, "Come to terms with your opponent or you will be handed over to the judge and thrown into prison. You will not get out until you have paid the last penny." The word "opponent" (antidiko) is likely a reference to the devil (see the same word for devil in 1 Pet. 5:8) who is an accuser against man (c.f. Job 1.6-12; Zech. 3.1; Rev. 12.10), and God is the judge. If we have not adequately dealt with satan and sin in this life, we will be held in a temporary state called a prison, and we won't get out until we have satisfied our entire debt to God. This "prison" is purgatory where we will not get out until the last penny is paid.

Matt. 5:48 - Jesus says, "be perfect, even as your heavenly Father is perfect." We are only made perfect through purification, and in Catholic teaching, this purification, if not completed on earth, is continued in a transitional state we call purgatory.

Matt. 12:32 -- Jesus says, "And anyone who says a word against the Son of man will be forgiven; but no one who speaks against the Holy Spirit will be forgiven either in this world or in the next." Jesus thus clearly provides that there is forgiveness after death. The phrase "in the next" (from the Greek "en to mellonti") generally refers to the afterlife (see, for example, Mark 10.30; Luke 18.30; 20.34-35; Eph. 1.21 for similar language). Forgiveness is not necessary in heaven, and there is no forgiveness in hell. This proves that there is another state after death, and the Church for 2,000 years has called this state purgatory.

Luke 12:47-48 - when the Master comes (at the end of time), some will receive light or heavy beatings but will live. This state is not heaven or hell, because in heaven there are no beatings, and in hell we will no longer live with the Master.

Luke 16:19-31 - in this story, we see that the dead rich man is suffering but still feels compassion for his brothers and wants to warn them of his place of suffering. But there is no suffering in heaven or compassion in hell because compassion is a grace from God and those in hell are deprived from God's graces for all eternity. So where is the rich man? He is in purgatory.

1 Cor. 15:29-30 - Paul mentions people being baptized on behalf of the dead, in the context of atoning for their sins (people are baptized on the dead's behalf so the dead can be raised). These people cannot be in heaven because they are still with sin, but they also cannot be in hell because their sins can no longer be atoned for. They are in purgatory. These verses directly correspond to 2 Macc. 12:44-45 which also shows specific prayers for the dead, so that they may be forgiven of their sin.

Phil. 2:10 - every knee bends to Jesus, in heaven, on earth, and "under the earth" which is the realm of the righteous dead, or purgatory.

2 Tim. 1:16-18 - Onesiphorus is dead but Paul asks for mercy on him "on that day." Paul's use of "that day" demonstrates its eschatological usage (see, for example, Rom. 2.5,16; 1 Cor. 1.8; 3.13; 5.5; 2 Cor. 1.14; Phil. 1.6,10; 2.16; 1 Thess. 5.2,4,5,8; 2 Thess. 2.2,3; 2 Tim. 4.8). Of course, there is no need for mercy in heaven, and there is no mercy given in hell. Where is Onesiphorus? He is in purgatory.

Heb. 12:14 - without holiness no one will see the Lord. We need final sanctification to attain true holiness before God, and this process occurs during our lives and, if not completed during our lives, in the transitional state of purgatory.

[v] John 14:16

[vi] Matthew 22:14

[vii] Matthew 25:1-13, Luke 21:36, Mark 13:32-33, Matthew 26:41, Mark 14:38, 1 Peter 5:8, Corinthians 16:13, 1 Thessalonians 5:2, Psalm 39:4

[viii] Matthew 10:30, Luke 12:7

[ix] Job 14:5-7, Psalm 139:16

[x] Romans, 2:6

[xi] Matthew 22:14

[xii] Luke 12:58-59, Matthew 5:25-26

[xiii] 1 Peter 4:8

[xiv] Acts 2:42-47

[xv] Acts 5:15-16

[xvi] John 20:21-23

[xvii] THE COUNCIL OF TRENT, Session XIV
CHAPTER VIII: On the necessity and on the fruit of Satisfaction.
Finally, as regards satisfaction,—which as it is, of all the parts of penance, that which has been at all times recommended to the Christian people by our Fathers, so is it the one especially which in our age is, under the loftiest pretext of piety, impugned by those who have an appearance of godliness, but have denied the power thereof,—the holy Synod declares, that it is wholly false, and alien from the word of God, that the guilt is never forgiven by the Lord, without the whole punishment also being therewith pardoned. For clear and illustrious examples are found in the sacred writings, whereby, besides by divine tradition, this error is refuted in the plainest manner possible. And truly the nature of divine justice seems to demand, that they, who through ignorance have sinned before baptism, be received into grace in one manner; and in another those who, after having been freed from the servitude of sin and of the devil, and after having received the gift of the Holy Ghost, have not feared, knowingly to violate the temple of God and to grieve the Holy Spirit. And it beseems the divine clemency, that sins be not in such wise pardoned us without any satisfaction, as that, taking occasion therefrom, thinking sins less grievous, we, offering as it were an insult and an outrage to the Holy Ghost, should fall into more grievous sins, treasuring up wrath against the Day of wrath. For, doubtless, these satisfactory punishments greatly recall from sin, and check as it were with a bridle, and make penitents more cautious and watchful for the future; they are also remedies for the remains of sin, and, by acts of the opposite virtues, they remove the habits acquired by evil living.

Neither indeed was there ever in the Church of God any way accounted surer to turn aside the impending chastisement of the Lord, than that men should, with true sorrow of mind, practice these works of penitence. Add to these things, that, whilst we thus, by making satisfaction, suffer for our sins, we are made conformable to Jesus Christ, who satisfied for our sins, from whom all our sufficiency is; having also thereby a most sure pledge, that if we suffer with him, we shall also be glorified with him. But neither is this satisfaction, which we discharge for our sins, so our own, as not to be through Jesus Christ. For we who can do nothing of ourselves, as of ourselves, can do all things, He cooperating, who strengthens us. Thus, man has not wherein to glory, but all our glorying is in

Christ: in whom we live; in whom we merit; in whom we satisfy; bringing forth fruits worthy of penance which from him have their efficacy; by him are offered to the Father; and through him are accepted by the Father. Therefore, the priests of the Lord ought, as far as the Spirit and prudence shall suggest, to enjoin salutary and suitable satisfactions, according to the quality of the crimes and the ability of the penitent; lest, if haply they connive at sins, and deal too indulgently with penitents, by enjoining certain very light works for very grievous crimes, they be made partakers of other men's sins. But let them have in view, that the satisfaction, which they impose, be not only for the preservation of a new life and a medicine of infirmity but also for the avenging and punishing of past sins.

For the ancient Fathers likewise both believe and teach, that the keys of the priests were given, not to loose only, but also to bind. But not therefore did they imagine that the sacrament of Penance is a tribunal of wrath or of punishments; even as no Catholic ever thought, by this kind of satisfactions on our parts, the efficacy of the merit and of the satisfaction of our Lord Jesus Christ is either obscured, or in any way lessened: which when the innovators seek to understand, they in such wise maintain a new one be the best penance, as to take away the entire efficacy and use of satisfaction.

CHAPTER IX: On Works of Satisfaction.
The Synod teaches furthermore, that so great is the liberality of the divine munificence, that we are able through Jesus Christ to make satisfaction to God the Father, not only by punishments voluntarily undertaken of ourselves for the punishment of sin, or by those imposed at the discretion of the priest according to the measure of our delinquency, but also, which is a very great proof of love, by the temporal scourges inflicted of God, and borne patiently by us.

xviii Ephesians 6:16

Manufactured by Amazon.ca
Bolton, ON

18989491R00046